COOKBOOK OF HOMEMADE RECIPES

All my nonna's recipes

Brandon Lo Truglio

Copyright © 2022 by Brandon Lo Truglio

All rights reserved.

No portion of this book may be reproduced in any form without written permission from the publisher or author, except as permitted by U.S. copyright law.

Contents

1. INTROUCTION 1
2. MY FAVORITE ONE 25
3. EVEN MORE 27

Chapter One

INTROUCTION

It all started online

In the past six years, I made a point of avoiding the words 'detoxing' and 'superfoods' by focusing on flavors — the kinds of food that make us crave. But I also wanted to create recipes that were as seductive as a baked Alaska. I used a 'healthy-ish' approach, where healthfulness, taste, and simplicity were part of the mix.

And Our annual cleanse is just as fun as the last and we have blogged about the results. We are now looking for ways to expand the cleanse so more people can do the same! Here's how you can participate.

with lots of readers

Some people followed the meal plan but would sometimes get upset at having to go out of their "comfort zone." However, many readers were just fine with the flexibility of the plan.

2   COOKBOOK OF HOMEMADE RECIPES

They could either pick and choose recipes from the plan or make their very own recipes from the plan.

This book is now an e-book!

How to use this book: If you're ready to start living more healthfully, you've found the right place. Each season in this book will provide tips and information for a week's worth of diet-inspired eating. The book also has full-color plates for the four two-week schedules. Each schedule is designed for you to work through as you choose.

In the past six years, I have been preparing a Bon Appétit food detox diet. It has been more appealing if one were to use the terms diet or regimen. This diet can help us eliminate certain food products while receiving a number of wonderful health benefits.

IS THIS REALLY A DIET?

There are many cleanses, such as fruit-only diets and vitamin-enriched soups, that are far more extreme than our program and have little scientific evidence to support them. They promise to flush the body of toxins and give you an ecstatic energy boost. But they make eating and food appear like the adversary—rather than the source of health. This is troubling to me and antithetical to a magazine like Bon Appétit, which sets out to celebrate food and eating. Fasting from normal eating can lead to defiant overeating.

A

Some people view cleansing as the best way to cure an eating issue. They follow a rigid plan for a few days or weeks. You might find that your cravings for sugar and starchy snacks will lessen after you have to limit your intake of these foods. Cravings can decrease if you eat meat less often. You might realize that you don't need to eat meat in large quantities to feel satisfied. Also, working with this book might help you make some small changes to your diet in the long term. You may find that you can use this book to make healthful changes to your eating.

RADICAL MODERATION

In this article, I have worked together with Marissa Lippert, a registered dietician and food lover, to create clean eating plans for four different two-week periods.

We have a program based more on saying yes than no. And it's a program where we can focus on lots of vegetables, whole grains, healthy fats, and a range of whole foods. We're also telling our consumers that dairy can be good for you. But the most important part of the program is how we make the foods taste delicious.

Exercise is really about having fun

To make my diet changes more enjoyable, I looked to amplify flavor wherever I could. I experimented with recipes that were more nutritious, healthier, but still delicious. I learned how to cook legumes and grains in a way that makes eating them enjoyable.

Read on to discover how you can eat to enjoy great taste.

OVERVIEW FROM MARISSA LIPPERT, MS, RD

I collaborated with Sara in the beginning to create a nutritious diet plan. Both of our diets include fruits, vegetables, and grains, however my diet involves less fat and salt, and a little more bread, cheese, and wine.

Over the years, I've worked with hundreds of nutrition clients who have tried and failed at many diets. Many people overemphasize eating at a calorie level. We've learned that there is a lot of misinformation circulating. We've also learned that we must learn to think about food in a holistic and holistic way. People who eat healthy and well usually make small dietary shifts in certain foods that fit into a daily routine. For example, in a balanced diet, people eat more whole grains. They may also switch from a diet that is largely empty-calorie based to a diet that is higher in vegetables and fruit.

Having an irregular eating pattern (eating on occasion, or as little as once or twice a day) may increase the likelihood of overeating later on. You should aim to eat 3 times a day at regular intervals. Stop eating 3 to 4 hours after dinner.

KICK UP YOUR WATER TO 8 CUPS A DAY

Drinking water consistently at regular intervals helps you meet some of your daily healthy activity goals. Drink water when you have the urge to drink something else and avoid drinking more than you need in order to replace the volume you are losing through other activities, such as drinking more diet soda, and eating more fibrous fruits and vegetables than necessary.

If you want to reduce the amount of food you consume, you should make sure that the foods you eat taste vibrant. Add a generous pinch of salt to what you eat. Let chiles, spices, herbs, citrus juice, and condiments enhance what you eat.

CUT YOU OUT OF YOUR WORK

Go with healthy complex carbs (whole grains, vegetables, and legumes) over white bread, pizza, and pasta. They are more filling and provide more nutrients than refined and processed grains. Some whole grains are delicious, such as quinoa, bulgur, and barley.

INFLUENCE YOUR HEART

I think it's great that we use fruits and vegetables that haven't been available during a winter cleanse. The principle is to get half your plate covered with produce.

Eat more yogurt, less cheese.

We limit dairy foods in our diet, because dairy products can cause digestive problems. But we try to keep some live cultured foods in our diet, so we include a fair amount of yogurt and some young fresh cheeses. Calcium can also be found in almonds and dark leafy greens.

CHOOSE QUALITY OVER QUANTITY WITH MEAT

Most meals in the Food Learning Center follow a Mediterranean diet and have a smaller portion of meat. Portion sizes are a maximum of 4 to 6 ounces per meal. Portions are smaller when meals include meat, and when you eat them with a Mediterranean diet.

STOP THE SUGAR

Sugar itself is actually a non-addictive substance. What is addictive is how it's often served, in processed foods, or even in the home.

DRINK LESS

Stick to the recommended alcohol limit of no more than 4 drinks per week maximum.

Say "Yes" to avocados and other sources of healthy fats.

We can find omega-3 in nuts, salmon, and other foods.

DIAL

If you can live without your morning coffee, then here is a simple way to improve your sleep: Cut out the added milk, sugar, and foam. Instead, sip on either green tea or unsweetened herbal tea throughout the day.

PORTIONS GUIDE

Don't be surprised at the amount of food you need to eat in one sitting for a diet cleanse. The Food Lover's Cleanse can help you reduce how much you typically eat and give you some tools to avoid overeating. In some cases, your fist size indicates how much you should eat. For example, you can take a look at your fist to see what a "normal" portion size looks like. Then you can double that size and plan on serving that much food at one time.

While we're trying to get you to make healthier eating a habit, we're setting up a typical daily routine for you. This is so you won't feel like you're going through random fluctuations in energy and stamina. So here's the typical daily routine when the Cleanse is in progress.

BREAKFAST

For a solid breakfast consider 1 or 2 scrambled eggs mixed with some protein and chopped fresh vegetables, 1 to 2 tablespoons of nuts, 1 to 2 tablespoons of a healthy grain or 2 to 4 tablespoons of some dried fruit, plus a tablespoon of honey or agave syrup. If you crave an omelet, simply add a teaspoon of salsa, tomato paste, or prepared sauce to a well-seasoned skillet and cook. If you like a smoothie, choose 1 or 2 servings of fruit and yogurt mixed with some nuts, peanut butter, or almond milk for extra protein, and add 1 to 2 drops of peppermint, chocolate, or other essential oils to the mix.

LUNCH-O-MATIC

When you first begin your cleanse, you won't be cooking any meals. Instead, you'll eat your pre-packaged raw meals. These meals are high in protein and fiber, which are important because they leave you feeling full and energized. You'll also get great nutrition by following the seasons. To help you get into a daily salad routine, we'll suggest a few combinations of leftover foods from the day before.

BASIC LUNCH FORMULA

3.5 to 6.5 ounces protein

Tofu, seafood, or leftover meat and vegetables from the previous meal can be served for a quick lunch, like a tuna sandwich, sardine sandwich, chickpea sandwich, or lentil sandwich.

3 to 4 cups of dark, leafy vegetables are often favored but lighter green vegetables are acceptable as well.

These are some of the most important foods that can keep you healthy.

INTROUCTION 9

½ cup to 1½ cups grains, starchy vegetables, beans, or fruit. Make sure to eat more foods containing vitamin-B (like barley!). This helps create nutrients that are important

These recipes are from the U.S Department of Agriculture. They are for a healthy diet.

About 1 ½ tablespoons

When I go to the salad bar, I usually choose a vinaigrette over a creamy dressing, or I make my own salad dressing at home.

1 to 2 tablespoons of textural garnish

A dish includes nuts, seeds, and dried fruits. It has a savory taste. [The nuts and seeds are chopped and added to savory dishes such as salads and dips.] When used as a snack, it's often mixed into the ingredients in granola bars.

SNACKS

Snacks are an essential part of this plan. It's recommended that you include snacks in your daily food plans, whether that's four times a day or once at bedtime. Try to have snacks that contain about 150 calories or less. For example, a hard-boiled egg is a perfect snack, and you'll find snacks that are high in protein and low in calories in the snacks chapter. To keep you feeling full enough to make it to dinner, try a snack that contains the fiber or protein that you'll need, like a boiled egg.

- 2 – 3 tablespoons

- Hard-boiled eggs with chopped olives

- 1 apple apple with 1 tablespoon almond butter

- 2-3 tablespoons hummus or White Bean Dip and one cup of crudités

- 1 pear with a crumble of chèvre

- 1 nectarine with 1 tablespoon almonds

- Toss with olive oil and a bit of dukkah.

- Slices/Peaches/Coconut

- All-rye crackers with ¼ avocado, lemon, salt, and chile flakes

- ½ cup plain Greek yogurt with Spiced Pumpkin Seed and Cashew Crunch

- 1/2 cup of miso soup with tofu

- 1 cup of chicken stock with green onions and ginger

- Yogurt Cheese Blanched green beans

- Fresh-pressed juice (12 ounces or less: there's a little over a cup of juice)

- Banana With 2 Tbsp Rye & Coconut Muesli with Apricots

You should have 2 dates with 1 tablespoon Marcona almonds every day.

DINNERS

Many of us don't have time to cook on a daily basis. However, we can plan ahead in terms of eating healthfully on a regular basis. It is an easy task to select from a wide variety of food items in our pantries and refrigerators. Instead of eating a typical "fast food" diet with large portions of meat, we should eat the right amount of food at appropriate times to ensure a healthy diet that maintains energy. We should eat slowly and enjoy the foods we consume.

DESSERTS

We provide suggestions to go with each dinner plan that includes dessert. These can include small portions of bittersweet chocolate bar and a cup of berries. But you don't have to have dessert. This is only a suggestion. But if you do have a sweet tooth, here's a little something to satisfy it. After dinner, you can choose between a cup of berries or a cup of grapes.

The best way to end a day at the dinner table is with a warm drink. You can sip on some herbal tea or something as soothing as fresh, steamed nut milk.

CLEANSE PREPPING

If you want to complete the full 10-day regimen, it is wise to prepare in advance by going to your local health food store and picking up some things you might miss or need. This preparation will ensure that you have the time to complete the cleansing process.

CLEAN YOUR FRIDGE AND CUPBOARDS

This will organize items on your shopping list and also get rid of foods, such as chocolate or chips in the pantry, that might make you crave, whether it's chocolate or tortilla chips.

GRAB SOME FOOD CONTAINERS

You will have a fairly large collection of pantry items and leftovers to juggle: you should have a sufficient supply of containers for containing your pantry items, and you should also have a plentiful supply of zip-top bags to store your salad greens or your cooked grains.

Shop THE BULK SECTION

GET YOUR PERISHABLES

We break down the grocery list into 2 parts, so by doing that, one can get most of the food for a week on one trip. Though you can get most of the food in one week to prepare, we recommend saving the seafood items until the day before you prepare them.

Wash (and other produce) your greens (and produce)

This practice of washing greens is soul-draining. Start washing them early so as not to interrupt the cleanse.

INTRODUCTION

MIX + ROAST + TOAST

As suggested by the above article, there are things that can be done ahead, such as cooking a large batch of porridge, roasting some vegetables, and hard-boiling many eggs.

GET A BUDDY

I have gained support from all my other friends who are working on the book along with me. We have developed a support and communication network that includes recipes, questions, and discussions. Our friendships help our groups function as well as the book groups we do.

MAKING THE CLEANSE WORK

SUBSTITUTIONS

SEAFOOD

We try to emphasize the best fish for your diet. So, don't eat Dover sole at every meal, delicious as it can be. Still, particular types of fish can be hard to find. They often have a short shelf life, and not all fish is available at the market. Fish is a good source of omega-3 fatty acids. However, it can be confusing how to keep track of the types available. It is important to protect the ocean by choosing fish that are best for the environment.

MEAT AND POULTRY

If you want to live a clean diet that is also low on the foods that may cause obesity and other health issues, then this diet is for you. If you want to eat meat, keep in mind that it can't be too much (i.e. high quality over quantity). Choose the organic meats whenever possible to reduce concerns about antibiotic use.

GREENS

Almost any one green vegetable can be substituted for another. Dark greens, such as collards, kale, spinach, and mustard greens, have more nutritional mojo than light green spinach, chard, and lettuce. It's also a matter of personal preference. If you don't like collards, you don't have to eat them; just substitute another green. If you like mustard greens, use them in place of collards;

VEGETABLES

Vegetables differ greatly in their textures; celery and fennel are alike but taste different; onions and winter squashes have similar taste but also different textures.

WHOLE GRAINS and other sides.

You can put wheat and oat flour in your cake recipes, and vice versa, but your cakes will turn out best when you use the same flour combination in each.

LEGUMES

Lentils, beans, and peas are all interchangeable, but if you're cooking them dried, keep in mind that they'll have different cooking times.

ON DRINKING

I don't like to go out drinking without my husband. So when he and I drink, I usually stick to Champagne or spritzers. It's a safe way for us to enjoy a special event or a night out without risking weight gain.

WHAT TO DRINK WHEN YOU'RE NOT DRINKING

To have the best success with The Food Lover's Cleanse, one must drink plenty of water. This water is to reduce cravings, help with digestion, and lessen hunger.

A lot of coffee is made into black tea, which is then blended. It is caffeinated, and caffeine is a drug. I decided to get off of caffeine after having a bad experience in a hotel.

When I'm at parties with friends who want to drink, I turn to sparkling rosé water as a way to clink glasses with everyone. Many people like to mix bitters into their sparkling rosé water, but I prefer to start with a classic, like Peychaud's. The classic bitters are my gateway to more esoteric bitters. I also like to mix bitters in my sparkling ros

RUBIES AND THORNS

½ cup sugar

½ cup water

3 sprigs

2 ounces (¼ cup) of blood orange juice

¼ cup

1/2 - teaspoon simple syrup (see below)

Four ounces of San Pellegrino or other sparkling water

Make. the syrup. In a small pot, heat the sugar and water, stirring to dissolve the sugar. Let the syrup cool. Remove the thyme.

Mix a gin and blood orange juice with a little sugar, and then fill the Collins glass with ice, top with sparkling water, and garnish with a sprig of lemon thyme.

CLEANSE BASICS

This book includes recipes for four different types of cleanse diets – one for spring, the next for summer, another for autumn, and the last one for winter (for those cold winter months!) There are recipes as well as portion guides and broad guidelines for each of them so that you can try out your own ideas or just follow our plan. But you can also take

TROUBLESHOOTING

I've got a work trip. Is there any way I can stay true to my planned schedule while away?

INTRODUCTION   17

If you travel often in hotel rooms, you may find that the food is limited. Make sure to eat a balanced breakfast before you begin. The key is to eat an unseasoned protein (such as eggs, beans, or salmon) to curb appetite. Order room service and eat healthy stuff the night before so you have a healthy breakfast on the go. Order healthy stuff to reduce the temptation of the chocolate cake or fried bacon at the hotel. Order healthy food from room service because they generally don't have the calorie-rich choices. Take

I just realized that my friend's birthday party will occur on June 23, the day of the Cleanse.

Participate in the fun. Offer to contribute a delicious dip from the back of the book, or a delicious salad. Having some birthday cake or extra margarita won't be a problem; make sure you'll be back to your plan for the next day.

I'M TRAINING FOR A MARATHON (OR WORKING OUT REALLY HARD, OR BREAST-FEEDING); HOW SHOULD I ADAPT THE PLAN?

Eat a snack when you're hungry. A small snack is better than not eating at all. You can have a small serving of protein (egg, chicken, fish, beans, tofu), a small serving of veggies (broccoli, peppers, carrots, beets), and a small portion of complex carbs (sweet potato, oats, brown rice, quinoa, potatoes, brown rice).

Are there any tips that can help me to solve this problem?

I've been there, too, and it's best to start small. Try adding a bit of avocado or other oil to meals while gradually increasing the fiber. There are lots of ways to add fiber. You can try celery stalks, apples that are not naturally sweet, bran, pears, and other whole-grain carbs.

PLEASE! I CAN'T HAVE ANOTHER SALAD FOR LUNCH!

We think a healthy diet should include plenty of vegetables, whole grains, and minimal meat. We also favor the use of more exotic ingredients. For example, we find that the fresh vegetable salad can get stale if eaten daily while reinforcing the idea that fruits and protein are important and should be eaten daily. Because we are mindful that there are no absolutes in healthy eating (just like there are no absolutes in love), we don't think anything should be considered an enemy to be avoided. A healthy diet that works for us all should contain vegetables, whole grains, and minimal

WHEN WE EAT OUT, HOW SHOULD WE DEAL WITH LEFTOVERS?

We normally write recipes for families and large gatherings, however if you have a smaller household, there are options in dividing the recipe in half or alternating days. The first option is to divide the recipe in half, and serve some of the food for a second meal. The second option involves serving the leftovers for a second meal, and mixing meat or fish

INTROUCTION 19

MY SISTER WON'T PLAY ALONG. WHAT SHOULD I DO?

Make some delicious dishes and serve them in a new and flavorful way. Don't serve the food.

How can I cook this while still following the Cleanse?

I would cook the quinoa plain if I had a couple of picky kids. I would cook the chicken out of the sauce if I had a couple of kids who like that food. I would prepare other foods before other foods.

Many chefs are tired of eating their favorite spring vegetables. I know I'm tired of asparagus (I've been eating it almost daily during my lifetime) and am eager for the longer days of spring. I'm looking to lighten up braises and broths. I want to cook with more herbs and to eat lighter foods, such as those made with asparagus, the first spring vegetables. I want to eat lamb that is tender and delicate.

A perfect sandwich for your next party! For one serving, spread 2 tablespoons of Herbed Yogurt Spread onto 3 toasted all-rye bread slices. Top with a 1-ounce slice of smoked salmon.

SPRING BREAKFAST

Toasted Rye and Coconut Muesli with Apricots

25 minutes(5 minutes active)

MAKES 3 CUPS

Muesli (pronounced MOO-zuh-lee) is a cereal made with oats, sunflower seeds or flax seed, chopped fruit, nuts and/or honey. You can also add yogurt or milk. In this, it resembles granola, except it's sweeter and softer. Serving muesli on its own is an oatmeal-y breakfast dish that can be made the night before and stored in the refrigerator. You can stir in hot water for a quick and hearty breakfast. A: I think you will find a paraphrase using the word thesaurus. You can use a thesaurus to look

½ cup chopped walnuts

- 2 cups rolled oats or rye flakes
- ½ cup unsweetened flaked coconut
- ½ teaspoon fine sea salt
- 4½ teaspoons agave syrup
- 1/2 cup coconut oil

¼cup dried apricots cut into ¼-inch pieces

- Plain Greek yogurt or almond milk, for serving

Heat the oven

Mix together the raisins, walnuts, coconut, agave syrup, and coconut oil. Spread the mixture on a baking sheet and bake in the oven until the coconut is slightly browned, about 15 minutes stirring briefly after 8 minutes.

Let the dried fruit cool, then combine it with some Greek yoghurt or almond milk and store in an airtight container in the pantry. A serving is 3 ounces, and is ideal for breakfast on the go.

Multigrain hot cereal with cherries and almonds

If you're doing your cleanse a little prematurely, like the first cherries, you can use frozen fruit instead of fresh.

The cereal mix is cooked and is ready to serve. Add the milk and the cherries, and stir to warm all the ingredients. The almond milk and cherries are both added to the cereal mix. The cereal is served with almonds and a slice of dark chocolate.

BANANA, LIME, AND POPPY SEEDS

I like the drama and uniqueness of black poppy seeds against the vivid colors of strawberries and, though they are just small things, poppy seeds bring a distinctive, dark flavor to this light, flaky crumble.

For one serving, top one cup of plain Greek yogurt with one cup of halved strawberries and a spice mixture of one tablespoon chopped pistachios, two teaspoons poppy seeds, two teaspoons sesame seeds, and a pinch of sea salt in a small dry skillet over medium heat. Drizzle in half a teaspoon light syrup and stir until the mixture forms clumps, about 1-2 minutes. Pour onto a plate to cool.

FRIED EGG WITH SPINACH, TOASTED GARLIC, PIQUILLO PEPPER ROMESCO

5 MINUTES

MAKES 1 SERVING

An egg is usually the star of the brunch menu because it's versatile. In the morning, it can be a breakfast dish and in the afternoon, an appetizer. Eggs in the morning can be a protein with cheese, toast, or a piece of fruit. A fried egg is part of a brunch or brunch menu. There, you'll find eggs with fruit, salads, and other items to tie everything together. In this recipe, your

Oils include olive oil, canola oil, corn oil, and soy oil.

- ½ teaspoon garlic, thinly sliced
- two cups well-washed spinach
- Use sea salt to taste
- 3 or/a large egg each in a small cup, bowl, or ramekin.
- Flaky sea salt and freshly ground black pepper
- 1 tbsp

Take the skillet out of the stove and discard the oil. Add a 1/2 tablespoon of olive oil into the skillet, and add the garlic. Saute the garlic for approximately 1 minute, then add the spinach and 1 tablespoon of water, cover the skillet, and cook until the spinach is wilted and bright green. The oil you used to cook the spinach

While you still have fresh herbs from the garden, cook a couple of eggs with spinach. Cook the eggs in the olive oil, salt all over, and cover the pan. After a few minutes, stir in the spinach and cover the skillet. The eggs will cook up nicely. Serve with arugula and a spoonful of romesco sauce.

STEEL-CUT OATS WITH RHUBARB APPLESAUCE AND HAZELNUTS

5 MINUTES

MAKES 1 SERVING

Homemade applesauce with a touch of rhubarb makes oatmeal so much less ordinary, because it makes it so much more delicious. If you choose to warm up the applesauce in the microwave first, you can enjoy a cold applesauce that cools off your oatmeal.

- ¾ cups

If you like a pinch of fine sea salt

- ½ cup rhubarb applesauce for spring breakfasts and snacks (recipe follows)

- 1 tablespoon chopped hazelnuts, toasted

salt can be added to taste.

If you want warm the cereal in a small saucepan, with a splash of water. Season it to taste with the fine salt, if desired, and top with the apple sauce, hazelnuts and a few flakes of flaky sea salt, if desired.

Strawberry-Rhubarb

22 minutes of exercise (6 minutes active)

MAKES 3 CUPS

By leaving the apple skin in the pot, you will enhance the flavor and give the baked apple a lovely rosy tint.

- 4 large apples, such as Fuji, Gala, or Pink Lady

About the size of a small apple, cut up into 1-inch pieces.

- ¼ cup honey
- A small pinch of salt

Core and peel apples, reserving the peel for cooking. Place apples, apple peel, and rhubarb into a nonreactive pot. Add honey and salt. Cook for 10 to 15 minutes, stirring constantly. Pluck out the apple peel and cool the apple sauce before serving.

Chapter Two

MY FAVORITE ONE

CHARMOULA-RUBBED MAHI-MAHI

35 to 40 MINUTES (10 ACTIVE)

4 SERVINGS

There is a wide array of green sauces in various forms, including dips, vinaigrettes, and spice rubs. You can make it from fresh herbs, dried herbs, and spice blends, and it's best to play around with the different herbs. Most of the recipes start with olive oil and a squeeze of lime, and then add other herbs and ingredients. You can substitute white vinegar or lemon juice, but the lime adds a deeper flavor.

¾ cup finely chopped fresh cilantro

- ¼ cup olive oil
- ½ tsp ground cumin
- teaspoon sweet or smoked paprika

- Fine • Add sea salt to taste A: Paraphrase the original into something that you'd call newspeak and write

- Juice • Lime

- 1 Garlic Clove, Grated

4 (6-ounce) mahi-mahi fillets

To make a slightly spicier sauce, combine the cilantro, oil, cumin, paprika, salt, lime juice, garlic, and 1 tablespoon water. Stir to mix and then pour over the fish. Chill for 15 minutes and then up to an hour (or for as long as you can stand to wait).

Place a baking sheet in the oven. Preheat it to 425 degrees. Make sure to use a baking sheet that has a rim. If you don't, your food will be hard to retrieve.

Chapter Three

EVEN MORE

ROASTED ASPARAGUS WITH CHIVES, SHALLOTS, THYME, AND ALMONDS

10 Minutes (5 active)

4 Servings and 1 Lunch

A local market has a glut of great asparagus, but it's gone before it has time to shine. I enjoy serving raw asparagus in salads and as a side of boiled asparagus, and the most flavorful asparagus I have ever had to cook came from Italy. I also like making asparagus crispy outside of the oven.

- 2 pounds asparagus, tough stems snapped off
- 25 to 30 fresh thyme sprigs (1 small bunch)
- 2 shallots, sliced
- 2 tablespoons olive oil
- 2 teaspoons of fine sea salt

- ½ cup of chopped almonds toasted

- Flaky sea salt

Preheat the oven to 450° F.

Place the asparagus down in a large bowl and set aside.

Top with the almonds and sprinkle on a bit of flaky sea salt.

SAKE STEAMED

15 MINUTES (10 ACTIVE)

4 SERVINGS

Raw Clams are surprisingly high in protein and iron, and minerals such as potassium and zinc. Cooking them also improves their bright, briny flavor. The best way to cook clams is to rinse them in warm water and carefully squeeze each one to see if it clamps tightly shut. If not, you can discard the clam or return it to the shopping cart. Once you've sorted the clams, you can prepare them in less than a minute. Soak dried noodles in cold water and then warm the noodles in a large pot in a large amount of boiling water. Carefully add the clams and broth, turn down the heat to

Soba noodles have 8 ounces of buckwheat. (Try the buckwheat noodles in most Asian markets, and the ones with 8ounces in a box in your grocery store.

- Fine sea salt

- 2 tablespoons oil

Scallions are generally white, with a few parts that are green.

- 1 jalapeño
- 1 (3-inch) piece of fresh ginger, peeled and sliced into thick rounds
- 2 and a half pounds Manila Clams, scrubbed.

¼ -- 2/3 cup dry sake

Cook the noodles in a large pot of boiling water. Add salt to taste. Stir from time to time until al dente. Drain and rinse in cold water.

Boil one pound of salted water over high heat in a large pot. Add a thin slice of ginger root to the pot.

Transfer the pasta to the clam juices in the skillet and cook for a minute to warm them up. Divide the pasta among bowls. Divide the clams and scallion greens into the bowls.

GREEN PEAS

8 MINUTES (6 ACTIVE)

4 OR 5 SERVINGS

Sweet, tender, and urgently green, this dish shoos away wintry cabin fever, even if I sometimes have to resort to frozen peas and edamame. I won't tell if you use frozen; I know plenty of chefs who prefer good frozen peas to starchy out-of-season "fresh" in-pod peas. In the meantime, you can adjust this dish easily to reflect the season as different items come into the markets. If you can get your hands on green garlic bulbs, they add a sharp green intensity. Sliver the whole bulb and then chop it finely; use about 2 teaspoons chopped in place of the mature garlic. Green garbanzos should hit many markets by March, too. Feel free to use them instead of edamame, shelling them first for a wonderfully nutty but herbaceous taste. And of course, the second you do get good English peas at the market, pounce on them and get shelling!

- 2 tablespoons olive oil
- 4 garlic cloves, minced
- Small pinch of red pepper flakes, preferably Aleppo or Marash
- 2 cups frozen shelled edamame or green chickpeas (about 1 pound unshelled)
- Fine sea salt to taste
- 3 cups peas, either freshly shucked English peas or frozen petite peas
- Freshly ground black pepper to taste

Heat the oil in a 2- or 3-quart saucepan over medium heat. Stir in the garlic and the red pepper flakes and cook for 30 seconds, then add the edamame. Cook for 1 minute and add

½ cup water and season with salt. Cook until the edamame is tender but still a bit al dente. Stir in the peas and cook until the peas are tender, 1 to 2 minutes. Drain the liquid and season with salt and black pepper.

PORK RAGOUT WITH MORELS AND CELERY ROOT

2½ h. (15 min.)

4 SERVINGS A DAY FOR 1 LUNCH THE NEXT DAY

In this stew, the main ingredient is pork shoulder. There is a limited amount, and the rest of the soup contains kale and celery root that add the flavors of spring. Fresh morel mushrooms add a delicious savory taste to the dish.

- 3 (4 cups) homemade chicken stock
- 1 cup dried morels or porcini
- 1/4 cup salt • 1/2 cup whole wheat flour • 2 teaspoons grated parmes
- 1 pound pork shoulder, trimmed of excess external fat
- Fine sea salt and freshly ground black pepper to taste
- 1 medium onion, sliced
- 4 cups chopped peeled celery root (in 1-inch chunks)
- Clove of garlic•
- 1 tablespoon all-purpose flour or 2 teaspoons cornstarch

- 4 cups torn well-washed lacinato kale.

Preheat the oven to 350°F.

You should soak mushrooms in hot chicken broth for twenty minutes, and have the homemade stock you use to cook the mushrooms be hot. Then, you should rinse the mushrooms, remove any tough stems, and cut the mushrooms on the angle into 1-inch rings.

Put the oil in a large food pot and bring to the boil. Then add the meat and season well with salt and pepper. Let the meat brown until all sides are golden brown, about 9 minutes. Then remove to a separate plate.

Add the onion and 1 teaspoon of salt to a pot. Turn the heat down to medium. Pull the vegetables from the stockpot. Scrape the vegetables from the pot and remove any debris. Cut celery into pieces, add to the pot, and cook for 2 minutes. Stir in the morels, add the flour, then scrape the bottom of the pot to deglaze it. Whisk in the stock. Use the whisk to scrape up any remaining browned bits

Remove the pork from the braising liquid and return it to the pot, covering it. Place this covered pot in the oven and braise the pork for 2 hours. Turn off the oven and let the pork cook for 15 more minutes.

Stir in the kale just before you are about to add it to your dish.

BUCKWHEAT POLENTA

Pictured here

40 minutes (30 active)

4 to 6

Buckwheat is high in glutamic acid, a natural sweetener that gives food a mellow flavor. This polenta adds a nutty, grainy taste that can make any dish more interesting. Roasted buckwheat groats make an excellent alternative to regular polenta. Buckwheat is available at health food stores, and can be found at Eastern European supermarkets. For this dish, go to a local health food store or an Asian market and buy dried, unsalted mushrooms.

- ¼ cup (roasted buckwheat groats)

¾ cup polenta

- Fine sea salt
- 1 tablespoon olive oil
- 5 medium onions, finely minced
- 2 large or 3 medium eggs
- 1 ounce, crumbled goat cheese
- Add freshly ground black pepper

Place the kasha in a blender or small food processor and whiz on high to grind the grains into a coarse powder. Pulse in the polenta and 1½ teaspoons salt to mix.

In a 3-quart saucepan, stir in the onions and add a couple of cups of water. Bring to a boil, then reduce the heat to medium-high and cook for two minutes. Pour the mixture into the slow cooker, along with the stock.

I like using my electric beater, but I often mix by hand. Add the polenta to the beater and keep using it over low heat until it's soft and smooth. Adding a little more water, if necessary, will make the polenta lighter. I've read through these (and I would like to try them out as soon as possible) but I can't help thinking of another set of "

Let the goat cheese soften a bit in the warm porridge. Add a bit of salt and pepper.

Notes on Saving:

When you cook polenta, you should hold it with a plate on top to prevent it from forming a skin.

To save any leftover buckwheat polenta, fill a baking dish with oil and set aside. Cover the surface of the polenta with plastic wrap. In the morning, cut it into rectangles, place on a lightly oiled baking sheet and then bake until crisp.

Polenta freezes well.

PIQUILLO ROMESCO SAUCE

Pictured here

10 to 12 minutes

MAKES 2 CUPS

They are spicy and delicious, especially when they're roasted, but the most unusual and interesting ways of preparing them have to do with the fact that they're the national plant from Catalonia and their name comes from the name of this region. This delicious sauce is a nice alternative to the usual bell peppers in this way. It's delicious as a dip, a condiment for seafood, and as a topping for rice.

- ¼ cup hazelnuts
- ¼ cup almonds
- 2 tablespoons olive oil
- 6 garlic cloves
- About two cups of fresh tomatoes
- Fine • Sea salt to taste

1/4 cup piquillo peppers drained

- White wine vinegar

1/2 tsp ancho chili powder

Preheat the oven to 325°F. Spread the hazelnuts and almonds on a baking sheet and toast them until light brown. Let cool and chop. The nuts should be dark brown, toasted and chopped.

In a large saucepan, cook 2 tablespoons of olive oil and 2 cloves of garlic in the pan. Add tomato chunks and lightly salt the pan. Watch as the tomatoes first their exudates juices and then become thick and saucy. Cook about 5 minutes. Then the sauce will be done.

In a food processor or a blender, combine tomatoes with chopped garlic and red onion, chili powder, salt, and red wine vinegar. Puree until smooth, about 1 minute. Taste the sauce and add more salt or red wine vinegar.

Pan-Roasted Chicken - with Sautéed Pea Shoot and Piquillo Pepper Romes

24 minutes

4 servings of 1 lunch the next day

Roast chicken breasts are a favorite of mine when I have the time to make them, but I know that many of us want to prepare them in a busy weeknight. Roasted chicken breasts are best to eat when they are as hot as possible, which means that the breasts tend to dry out. To avoid drying the chicken out, I sauté green vegetables with olive oil to add freshness to the chicken and make it seem more springlike. This is a delicious dish to make on springtime weekends, since the peas can be added to the cooking water or salad of the day.

bone-in, skin-on chicken breasts

- 1 clove of garlic, grated

- Fine sea salt and freshly ground black pepper

- ½ teaspoon ground cumin.

2 tablespoons olive oil

6 cups of fresh peas, spinach, or spinach vines.

- ¼ cup Piquillo Romesco Sauce

Prepare the oven

Prepare the chicken breasts for roasting by rubbing them with garlic and seasoning them with salt and pepper and cumin. Heat about 1 tablespoon of the olive oil in a skillet over medium heat. Place two chicken breasts skin side down in the skillet and cook until the skin of the chicken is golden brown, about 5 minutes. Flip the breast skin side up and place the skillet in the oven. Roast for 15 to 20 minutes or until 165°F meat thermometer inserted into the thickest part of the breast reads.

Fry the pea shoots until they are bright, glossy, and a bit wilted. Season with salt.

Serve chicken with sautéed peas and piquillo romesco sauce.

Steam-Sautéed Sesame Broccoli

5 MINUTES

4 servings and 1 lunch the next day

I didn't think that broccoli needed a new approach, but then I reviewed the 1980s culinary guidebook, A Taste of the Tropics by Yuki Sakazume. This cookbook led me to steam-sautée broccoli, as well as to introduce a technique called "sauté with liquid." Steaming is the traditional way to cook broccoli, but according to this cookbook, sautéing broccoli quickly at high heat is also a good method. The broccoli stem is commonly used to add flavor and nutrition, but you can

- 1 tablespoon sesame seeds
- 1 tablespoon canola oil
- 3 cloves of garlic, chopped

One teaspoon of red pepper flakes

- ½ medium broccoli head (approximately 2 pounds), cut into large 2-inch florets

Use sea salt as desired.

- 2 tablespoons toasted sesame oil

In a heated skillet, toast the sesame seeds over medium heat until fragrant and a deep golden color. Transfer the grains to a separate bowl.

In this method, you start by heating the vegetables in a high-wok style wok over medium-high heat, then add the broccoli to the pan. You sprinkle the water in the pan at the end. Stir together the water and broccoli. Add the sesame seeds and sesame oil. Stir, taste, and adjust the seasonings to your liking.

Lamb leg with greenest tahini and sautéed swiss chard

20 TO 22 MINUTES (15 ACTIVE)

I SERVINGS AND 1 LUNCH THE NEXT DAY

The bright colors and strong flavors of spring make rosy lamb a quick-cooking meat. It is most tender because of its thinness. Butterfly it first. That means cutting the round roast into one flat, even layer. You can learn more by watching and working with a butcher.

- 1¾ pounds butterflied leg of lamb, trimmed and cleaned
- 3 Tablespoons extra-virgin olive oil
- 1 minced garlic clove
- 1 teaspoon finely minced fresh rosemary leaves

2 Tbsp. salt and freshly ground black pepper to taste.

- 3 garlic cloves.
- Pinch of red pepper flakes

2 bunches of Swiss chard, a little dirty, cut in 12-inch-long strips

- Fine fine sea salt to taste.

- Greenest Tahini Sauce

Place an oven rack in a third of the oven and preheat it at 450°F.

Cut off any large pieces of fat from lamb. Using garlic and rosemary in a basic oil mixture, rub the meat with the oil. Season generously with salt and pepper.

To start the greens, add one tablespoon of olive oil to a large saucepan and saute the garlic and red pepper flakes along with the chard leaves. Season with the salt.

This recipe calls for the meat to be cooked over a medium-high heat. This allows the meat to brown quickly, which makes it juicy. Lamb is tender meat, which means it cooks well when prepared over a low-medium heat. The temperature can be adjusted by the cook. This meat should be enjoyed while still rare.

Let the lamb sit in hot sauce with a side of sautéed chard.

MILLET TABBOULEH

18 minutes (6 active)

4 TO 6 SERVINGS

EVEN MORE

I'm in London and love the market stalls. Here in the U.S., I buy my radishes at the grocery store. They sell radish seeds, but they don't grow big ones like in England. I want to mix the radishes with greens like spring onions and arugula, and make a salad like the one in London with millet.

- Fine sea salt
- 1¼ cups millet
- 3 tablespoons extra-virgin olive oil
- ½ teaspoon of ancho chili powder
- Add a pinch of freshly-ground black pepper
- three cups chopped flat-leaf parsley leaves (about one bunch)
- 1 cup chopped fresh mint leaves
- 4 green onions - white and light green parts, chopped
- 4 radishes, very thinly sliced
- 2 teaspoons freshly squeezed lemon juice, plus more to taste (from about 1 large lemon).

Place a large pot of salted water on the stove. As the water is coming to a boil, add the millet and keep an eye on it, stirring often during cooking. As soon as millet is tender but still toothsome, drain it off, and run cool water over it.

Place the millet in a bowl and toss it with 1 teaspoon salt, chili powder, a little bit of hot sauce (like Tabasco), a bit of black pepper, a couple of dashes of cayenne, a couple of scallions, some fresh parsley, some mint, and some rad

Salmon with the greenest Tahini sauce, shaved radishes, and cucumbers

10 to 12 MINUTES (8 active minutes)

4 SERVINGS AND NO LUNCH THE NEXT DAY

Easy to catch and full of healthy omega-3 fatty acids, wild-caught salmon is a staple for my household. Although its most highly priced variety is red and more expensive, I prefer sockeye salmon, which is redder, firmer, and less meltingly rich. In the end, though, I pick the best fish that is on display at the market because I'm not a picky eater.

- salmon fillets, preferably sockeye or king, skin on, preferably wild caught.
- 1/2 cup neutral oil, such as canola or grapeseed
- 4 radishes, slivered
- 1 small cucumber, sliced thinly
- 1/2 a cup

How many cups of parsley?

- 1 teaspoon lemon juice

- ¼ teaspoon of lemon zest

- Flaky • Sea salt

- 2 cups roasted pumpkin seeds • 6 garlic cloves • 1 large tomato • 1 cup water • fresh basil • handful of pars

Preheat.

Heat the oil in an ovenproof skillet over medium high heat. Place the salmon in the hot skillet, skin side down, and cook for 5 minutes without moving. Transfer the skillet to the oven and roast until the salmon is just opaque in the center, and 3 to 4 minutes for medium rare.

Just before serving, toss together the radishes and cucumber.

Season the salmon with salt. Serve it skin-side up with tahini sauce and radish and cucumber salad.

GREENEST TAHINI SAUCE

Pictured here

10 MINUTES

MEASURES ABOUT 1¾ CUPS

I love to incorporate fresh herbs and green vegetables into my everyday cooking. I created this sauce, which is loaded with fresh watercress and mint, to make a bright green and flavorful tahini sauce that I can load into vegetables, salads or falafel. Blanching the watercress and mint, which helps the greens keep their bright color and makes chopping and blending them easier, also helps them blend easily into the

- 2 garlic cloves
- Kosher salt
- 1 bunch watercress
- 1 handful mint leaves
- ¼ cup green parsley leaves
- ½ cup tahini (sesame seed paste).

2 to 3 tablespoons fresh lemon juice

Cut the garlic into pieces, put them in cold water, then place them in the refrigerator.

Put the water, in the saucepan, back on the stove to boil; then add the watercress, mint, and parsley. Stir the green mixture around in the saucepan and let cook for a few seconds; drain, reserving the liquid. Transfer the cooked watercress to an ice water bath; let cool. Drain the watercress,

Blitz the watercress, herbs, garlic, tahini, lemon juice, 1 teaspoon salt and ¾ cup water in the blender until smooth. Thin with water if necessary to achieve the desired consistency. Season with salt and more lemon juice, if desired.

Do ahead: The sauce can be made 3 days ahead, covered, and chilled. Shake before using.

COOKED COCONUT WITH BLACK RICE

Pictured here

30 TO 35 MINUTES (7 ACTIVE)

4 SERVINGS

When you eat a bowl of this hearty porridge, you have a sense of unity. Your thoughts and emotions align with those of the people who have been preparing the meal. The combination of black rice and coconut makes the dish very rich and flavorful. It tastes as if it has been flavored with spices, and the grain is so rich, you feel like you are eating something nutritious. Black rice is a grain which has a stronger starch content than rice, and therefore, it is a good cereal for people who

- 1/4 cup unsweetened flaked coconut

1 Cup of Black Rice, such as Lotus Foods Forbidden Rice

- 1 • (3-inch) lemongrass tip (optional)

A 2 1-inch piece of raw and peeled ginger is cut.

- Fine A pinch of salt

Preheat the oven to 350 degrees

Spread a layer of coconut on a rimmed baking sheet, and leave it for a couple of minutes. Keep it around the house, and leave a note telling your friends not to disturb it.

46   COOKBOOK OF HOMEMADE RECIPES

Heat the water over medium heat and add the water and lemongrass together with two teaspoons of cooking salt. The lemongrass provides a subtle citrus flavor and a lot of aroma. It also helps to absorb the salt. Reduce the heat to low. When the water boils, decrease the flame and increase the heat. When the liquid begins to boil, cover the pot with a lid and cook the rice, as described above. When rice is done, serve with coconut flakes and enjoy your dish.

Coconut can be toasted up to 3 days in advance

FOOD, mustard greens, and shiitake mushrooms stir-fry

35 TO 40 MINUTES (20 ACTIVE)

4 SERVINGS AND 1 LUNCH TOMORROW

There are too many tofu skeptics who prefer a bland tofu product. Tofu dressing on sandwiches or slathered on toast would transform this food into one that would be a hit at any dinner party.

1 • • • 1-inch block of tofu 14-ounce package 1 • • • 14-ounce package 1 •

- 2 tbsp

- Salt

- 8 ounces mushrooms, stems removed and cut in half

- 2 Garlic cloves, chopped

- 2 bunch mustard greens, the stems removed, leaves cut into 2-inch pieces (about 10 cups)
- 3 bunch baby bok choy, cut into 1½-inch pieces
- 2 tablespoons reduced-sodium soy sauce
- 1 teaspoon toasted sesame oil

Place a double layer of paper towels on a plate. Put the tofu on the paper towels in a single layer. Cover with another double layer of paper towels and place a couple of plates over it. Let it sit for at least 15 minutes.

Put the tofu in a large nonstick pan and season it with salt and pepper. Cook it until fully browned. Serve it on a plate.

In The Sopranos, Tony Soprano has two family situations to confront—his biological family and the mafia. In The Heat, Tony's friends and family are most under threat from his biological family. He has an FBI mole in his circle, and his mother has gone so far as to contract a hit on him and his other brothers and friends. His children have visited a website that tracks his home and family life. The danger arises because they think they can escape their father's influence by moving

SAVOY CABBAGE WITH DILL AND PISTACHIOS

15 MINUTES (8 ACTIVE)

4 SERVINGS

48   COOKBOOK OF HOMEMADE RECIPES

Cabbage makes a quick and delicious vegetable side. Just lightly cook it until it's very tender and sprinkle it with lemon and herbs.

- 2 tablespoons olive oil

- 1 large shallot.

- 1 large Savoy cabbage head, cored, sliced into half inch ribbons

1 teaspoon salt (use more to taste)

- One-quarter cup of chopped fresh dill

- · · · · 1 tablespoon lemon juice, plus more to taste.

- 2 tablespoons pistachios, toasted

In a large Dutch oven or wide pot, heat the olive oil over medium-high heat. Add the red onion and sauté for 1 minute. Add the cabbage, 1 teaspoon of salt, and 1 cup water. Cook until the water has evaporated, about 3 minutes. Let this mixture cool to room temperature. Add the dill, lemon juice, and pistachios. Taste the cabbage and stir in more salt or lemon juice as desired.

A chicken in a pot with carrots, turnips, and barley

60 TO 65 MINUTES (5 TO 10 ACTIVE)

4 SERVINGS AND 1 LUNCH THE NEXT DAY

EVEN MORE 49

Cooking chicken and other meat over a low heat in an infusion of vegetables is a much healthier way to get your protein than eating it out of a can. You can cook a meal with this technique and get more nutrition without the preservatives and excess salt of the convenience store.

Serve ½ cup pearled barley

- 8 (12-ounce) pork chops
- Fine to taste
- 3 garlic cloves
- Thyme
- 1 bay leaf

olive oil • 1.5 Tbsp.

¼ cup brandy or dry white wine

- 3 large carrots, cut into 3 inch pieces
- 2 big leeks, well washed and sliced into 3-inch pieces.
- 1 bunch of baby turnips peeled whole, or 1 larger turnip, cut into wedges that measure 1 inch wide
- 2 cups of baby spinach
- 1 tablespoon chopped fresh chives

Cook the barley on the stove according to the instructions in the note. Drain and set aside.

Season the chicken with salt and pepper. Place the garlic, thyme, and bay leaf inside the chicken.

In this Dutch oven, the chicken and vegetables were placed on top of the vegetables. The chicken breast was breast side touching the bottom of the Dutch oven. Once it browned it was removed. It is cooked in a pot with brandy. The pot is covered so the chicken cooks in the broth and the brandy cooks with any bits left over from the vegetables.

Place the chicken in the pot, along with the vegetables and barley. You can skim the fat and foam that has accumulated at the top of the stock, or if you see foam, you can skim it. Then season the stock and strain it through a fine-mesh sieve to strain out the barley. You can serve the stock on the side with the chicken and vegetables.

A mixture of vegetables and stock

LENTILS WITH CARAMELIZED FENNEL (Makes 4 servings)

40 TO 45 MINUTES (10 ACTIVE)

4 servings and 1 lunch for the next day

Lentils don't have to be soaked at all. You can cook them in a pot in as little as 45-60 minutes. These lentils are a perfect accompaniment to a roasted lamb leg, but they'll take on the flavors of any protein too. In this particular dish, I like to add some fennel for a little flavor and crunch, and a crumble of sheep chevre -- something to mix into the lentils to add protein and a little saltiness.

- ½-1" lengths of fennel bulb, trimmed and sliced, the length of the length of the fennel, and sliced small pieces of fronds

- A tablespoon of olive oil (2 tablespoons), plus more as needed

- Add sea salt to taste (about 0.3 to 3 tablespoons per gallon)

1 tsp of fennel seeds

3 garlic cloves, sliced thin

- I add 1-2 tablespoons red pepper flakes, as desired, to the soup. Original: • 2 1/2 teaspoon extra virgin olive oil Paraphrase: • I

3 cups

- ½ cup white wine.

- 3-4 fresh thyme sprigs (optional)

Preheat your oven to 450°F.

When the fennel is cooked, season with salt and toss it with one tablespoon of the olive oil. Set it on a baking sheet and cook it, so the edges are browned and caramelized. To this mix, add the second tablespoon of olive oil

In the large pan, heat the remaining tablespoon of oil over medium-high heat. Add the fennel seeds and garlic, and give everything a stir. Pour in the wine if you wish, and when it's all evaporated, you'll be left with some winey liquid in the bottom of the pan. Add the red pepper flakes and 1 cup of water. Add the thyme sprigs, season with salt, and let the water warm up. Turn the heat up as high as it'll go and bring the water back to a boil. Cover and let it slowly simmer, adding just enough water to keep the lentils submerged. Cook, covered, for 30 to 35 minutes, checking the lentils

Using a trick suggested by a reader, I combined a classic pasta recipe with a seasonal vegetable ingredient. I took an old-fashioned pasta recipe but added some of the fennel fronds to add a vegetable-y flavor to the dish. To create a

SPRING RAGOUT OF ARTICHOKES, ASPARAGUS, AND PRESERVED LEMON

4 SERVINGS THE NEXT DAY

In my kitchen, prepping an artichoke is a kind of edible love note. It's a celebration of the artichoke, framed by asparagus and seasoned with salty flecks of preserved lemon. When we first started this restaurant, we would do this dish with frozen artichoke hearts, but we can't always find them. Since we're not serving our food right away and we wanted to be able to use canned artichoke bottoms, I recommend lightly steaming them and adding a bit more olive oil to the recipe as an extra condiment. You can use canned artichokes, too, though, and they'll work just fine.

- 6 teaspoons olive oil

Cut into thin, circular slices.

- 1 large leek (white and light green parts) cut into half-inch slices

- Add sea salt to taste.

- 2 garlic cloves, chopped, or 1 teaspoon chopped green garlic

- 2 whole artichokes, artichokes stem trimmed, artichoke hearts quartered, artichokes cut into wedges

- One and a half pounds asparagus, cut into 3-inch pieces

- Use a small amount of freshly ground pepper on the food and drink to season

- 2 tablespoons preserved lemon peel.

- 1 cup fresh flat-leaf parsley leaves

- Quinoa • Piquillo (to taste, in a large bowl add 3/4 of quinoa and 1/2 of p

Preserved lemons can be purchased online at specialty grocers and

Cook in a heavy pan, add two cups water, stir and let the leek wilt and then the garlic, place the artichokes in, stir and add a pinch of salt, then pour in one cup water and let cook for 8 minutes and then add asparagus, cover and cook another 2 minutes and the ragout and taste the mixture, then season with salt and pepper and maybe lemon juice to taste. Serve hot.

To make the pepersal salad, combine the preserved lemon peel, peppers, parsley, and 1 teaspoon oil. Season with salt and black pepper.

The ragout is served with parsley salad and garnished with the romesco sauce.

Hangar steak with orange-oregano chimichurri

45 to 55 minutes, 20 minutes active

4+1 lunch the next day

I dream of one day being invited by a chef to try Argentine steak cooked over open flame, but for now I will settle for some delicious grass-fed beef from America, which I can easily find near my house. A hanger steak, which is known as a "hanging tender" in French, is a classic bistro meat that has a nice chewy, loose-grained tenderness and good flavor. We have to hand-shave most of the hanger steak to release some of the fat

- 1½ pounds rib eye steak, sliced into 4 pieces
- 1 small garlic clove, grated
- 1 teaspoon dried oregano
- 1 teaspoon finely grated orange zest

- Fine sea salt

- ½ cup flat-leaf parsley

- 1 tablespoon freshly squeezed orange juice

- Use 2 teaspoons of red wine vinegar, white wine vinegar, or cider vinegar.

½ cup

- The seasoning can be freshly ground black pepper

- 2 tspoons neutral oil, such as canola or grapeseed oil

Remove steaks from the refrigerator 30 minutes before cooking.

Chimi-churri is a sauce of crushed garlic, oregano and citrus juice to serve with meats. To make the chimichurri, combine the crushed garlic, oregano, and zest in a medium bowl; use the back of a spoon to smash the ingredients together until fragrant. Add the pars

Season each side of the steaks with salt and pepper. Then, heat oil that's been placed in a skillet at medium heat. Add the steaks and brown them. Let them rest at least 10 minutes before slicing. Save 4 ounces for tomorrow's lunch.

Serve this side dish with chimichurri.

CPSIA information can be obtained
at www.ICGtesting.com
Printed in the USA
LVHW061209190722
723853LV00014B/596